Open The Fist

poems by

Elya Braden

Finishing Line Press
Georgetown, Kentucky

Open The Fist

ACKNOWLEDGMENTS

Thank you to the editors of the following publications, in which versions of
these poems originally appeared:

Algebra of Owls: "How to be Deposed"
Causeway Lit: "Overrun"
Cliterature: "What is the Truth?" under my nom de plume, E.B. Pearson
Euphony: "Now" (renamed "Woke")
Forge: "Asking for It"
Jewish Women's Literary Annual: "The Black Dress I Wore at My Sister's
    Wedding" (renamed "Whatever")
Linden Avenue Literary Journal: "Tethered"
Main Street Rag: "Yom Kippur"
Snapdragon, A Journal of Art & Healing: "When Joy Comes"
The Chiron Review: "Lessons from the Upper Realms," "Open House," and
    "Electric Hanukkiah in the Window"

Publisher: Leah Maines
Editor: Christen Kincaid
Cover Art: Elya Braden
Author Photo: Bader Hower Photography
Cover Design: Elizabeth Maines McCleavy

Printed in the USA on acid-free paper.
Order online: www.finishinglinepress.com
            also available on amazon.com

Author inquiries and mail orders:
Finishing Line Press
P. O. Box 1626
Georgetown, Kentucky 40324
U. S. A.

Table of Contents

Table of Contents

Your silence will not protect you.
~ Audre Lorde

To My Sisters in Incest I Need to Say

Love the body that is yourself.
Tender your fingers as you wander
the country for which there is no map
between the rise and fall of your legs.

Open into the mouth that kisses
your weeping. Open into the palm
that cools your forehead.

Open the fist that blacked your eye,
blued your jaw, purpled your belly.
Kiss it once, kiss it twice, kiss it
until the Judgment Day,

until the sun explodes,
until the fist remembers
it was once a father, an uncle,
a brother, a husband, a boy.

Open the door to your mother's bedroom
where she pillows herself in silence,
drapes herself in sleep,
forgets she has a daughter.

Do not barge in hurling trolls
and three-headed dogs. Do not
wear your wig of snakes. Do not
carry your executioner's ax.

Enter singing—a psalm or a
lullaby. Enter in feathers
and fur. Enter in the green
envelope of your birth.

Curl into the cradle of her body
until she remembers she was
once a mother, a daughter,
a child crying in the night.

Every night, chant prayers
for every daughter of this planet,
for every forsaken mother,
for every moon-cursed father
foaming at his leash.

Electric Hanukkiah in the Window

Mommy, I asked, *why do we put it in the window?*

To show our neighbors that we are not
drinking the blood of Christian children.
            I remember her answering.

Dark bird, she swooped around the kitchen
            in snug pedal-pushers,
her knuckled fingers busy—
            sprinkling cinnamon over a kugel,
            basting a pot roast,
only her bouffant hair shellacked into stillness.

But that can't be right.
I've twisted this recollection somehow.
It's Passover that recalls the blood,
            not of Christian children, but of lambs.

I remember those eight days of gifts,
            an annual competition
with our Christian friends to see who got
more loot at the end of the season.
But even daily gifts couldn't staunch my hunger
            for evergreen, incense, an angel.

Day one: a little Kiddle doll.
Day two: another.
Day eight: the big reveal—
            a Kiddle doll game board.
A joint present for me and my little sister.
With only 11 months between our births,
            it could only end in tears.

Who knows where it is now?
On the trash heap of time,
along with the electric Hanukkiah,
    our tired dreidels,
and the Alice in Wonderland sheets
stained in my memory
with midnight and father and blood.
    Or maybe, I've twisted that, too.

Woke

Like the gong of a bell in a Buddhist temple,
your mother's slap will wake you
out of the stumbling stupor
of your ten-year-old life,
wake you up to the *now*
of swallowed tears and weak ankles,
a ruby handprint rising
from the dough of your face
like a starfish reddening on the sand
under the sun's sightless stare,
your first glimpse of the Seawitch
skulking in the kelp-beds of the ocean-sharded eyes
of the dark-haired beauty you once called *Mommy*.

Later, you can scatter your mother's ashes
beyond the rim of tomorrow,
but her crusted waters will flow in you forever,
in the curve of your chin,
the way your smile lists to the right,
the deliberate loop of your cursive "g,"
and the memory of her once, long-ago slap
still ringing, ringing in your ears.

Appetites

The moths won't stop
            eating my shirts.
Their calling card:
a deranged bullseye,
            lacey archipelago
                        of absence.

They target the rise
of my tender belly,
            soft mound
I've warred with
            since my hips spread,
                        my bloods came.

For years, my mother
fought to rein in
            my wayward body,
force-feeding me
            cantaloupe
                        and cottage cheese.

Yet her "surprise weigh-ins"
could no more curb
            my stealthy midnight binges,
than my ducked chin could
save me from towering
in the back row
            of every school picture
                        until high school,

                or stop
my big brother's closed-door
investigations, leaving me
            as stained and holey
as my terra cotta tee
            stitched with hearts
                        and angel wings.

On every equinox and solstice
I replace my eco-friendly sachets
            of *Moth-Away* and
            respray my cedar chips
                        with eau d'forest,
yet with each new moon,
I tally my casualties:
plum silk blouse,
            blue batik shirt,
                        crimson tank top.

In my dreams,
            I'm terrorized
by a cacophony of
            minute mandibles sawing,
            teeny teeth gnawing,
                        gnawing, sawing, gnawing.

As if
a thousand tiny bites
            to the heart
of my own unending appetite
            could fill their constant need.

In My Father's Office

He was a smaller thing at home,
trapped on a concrete island
like the noon-dazed lion at the zoo.

The insistent swarm of our voices
pricked him awake. Head shake,
rise and roar: *"You idiot!" "Stop crying!"*
"I'll give you something to cry about!"

On special Saturdays, I was invited
to his glass and steel-girded castle—
all elevators, carpets, empty offices,
walls papered with pin-striped secrets.

Daddy's wide wood desk too polished
to touch, crisp folders set at right angles.
His leather chair on rollers: a throne for the king
of everything. His cup of pencils sharp as arrows,

hungry for blood. Lined up next to them,
the frozen smiles of our school pictures. This
is how he loved us: tidy, adoring, silent.

Whatever

I've parted ways with bridesmaid's dresses
as casually as with the brides who chose them:

the emerald-green moiré double-ruffled taffeta,
the peach sorbet silk ass-hugging skirt suit,
and the lace-collared navy-blue rayon Neo-Victorian,
I let my daughter slash and splash with fake blood
        to become the bride of Dracula.

I only kept this one dress—
from my sister, my only sister.
We'd had a competition to choose a dress
our bridesmaids would want to wear again.
She won—black velvet, Victor Costa,
sweetheart neckline, sarong skirt.
Elegant, sexy, sophisticated.
So her. So the girl I wanted to become.

At her wedding, the black velvet caressed
my November skin, whispering: *Touch me,*
but my sister, in snowy satin, was untouchable,
her favorite word: *whatever*
clandescing in her ice-blue eyes,
like a thorn concealed in the lush greenery
of her bouquet of crimson roses.

It was our sister dance—
I'd step forward, she'd step back,
mutter: *whatever* and *close the door*
on your way out, with a flick
of her wrist, as if my longing
for sisterhood was as over-blown
as the blushing cabbage roses on the chintz dress
I'd swooned over for *my* bridesmaids.

I imagine her discarding that dress, my dress,
the way she later discarded me,
when I took up too much room,
broke too many rules,
brought back too many memories.
But I still have her dress—
all black and velvet and vacant—
hanging in my closet.
Whatever.

Asking For It

I am shuffling down my office hallway, head bent, scanning pages,
bundled in blue jeans and a gray crew-neck sweater.

Summoned back after midnight on December 30th to document
a year-end acquisition. Sleep crusts my unmade eyes.

The discrete carpet expunges his footsteps. I think I'm alone
until his urgent lips pressed to my exposed neck jolt me awake.

I recoil as he breathes into my ear: *You are the sexiest woman
in this firm.* I thought he was a friend,

but this is no tender offer, no special motion, no appeal.
I hear no compliment in his words, only the echo

of my mother's blame: *Well, it wasn't really your brother's fault;
I remember you coming downstairs in a bikini when you were eight,
posing and saying: "Look at me, aren't I sexy?"*

What Is the Truth?

The truth is I blamed myself—
his sly fingers fluttering,
lick and tickle between my legs,
ephemera of pleasure.
Perhaps, if I had forced myself
to stare into the obsidian eyes
of the snakes twisting from his head,
and turned myself to stone, he would have
risen from my bed and left, defeated
as a grizzly abandoning a balled-up
prey, playing dead.

The truth is I'll never know
more than the splintered
flashbacks to that first ripping,
pelvis shrieking, my shattering—
like a ceramic planter knocked
from a wall, shards
and leaves exploding,
dirt everywhere, black
as my shame. My breath
sucked into a penny, choking
my throat, my mouth filled
with copper. Had I bitten
my tongue or inhaled the reek
of blood, blood between my legs,
and was it blood?

My eyes squinched shut,
purple, red and blue dots dancing
behind them, wetness
running down my thighs,
Oh, no, did I wet the bed?
Mommy will be so mad.
My breath, my breath.
His hand a tarantula over my mouth,
swallowing my prayer:
Please stop daddy, please.

My world shrunk to dancing dots,
to wet, to black, to splinters,
his voice the hiss
of a thousand snakes:
I will kill you if you tell.

The truth is I'll never know the truth,
never know whether my body broke
its silence after forty years
to deliver up a memory, the answer
to the questions that stitched
my life with mystery:
Why do I leap up in bed
when my hair, a blanket, or
my lover's hand brushes
my mouth? Why do I fear
the upstairs when I'm alone,
shutter every window, flashlight
every closet, clutch my phone?

Or is the truth, as my father claims:
You always had a vivid imagination.

Overrun

My body was a highway interchange.
    Father, brother, frat boy,
        preacher's son.

All the "no's" I couldn't say like nickels,
    dimes and quarters tossed
        into the pockets of my tollbooth.

People say I look like my mother, but my father's nose
    dominated my face until a doctor's
        hammer and file erased daddy's grip.

But I can't scrape his freckles from my arms.
    They lead me back to childhood—
        an atlas of fingerprints rising from my skin.

My mother met a woman she thinks
    is her half-sister, the legacy of her father's affair
        when she was 11. 11, my age when my father

scored with his office confidant and co-worker,
    when my parents threatened to divorce.
        Infidelity—is it a gene passed down to me?

Alone at the beach, I dream of my former lover
    kissing me in taxis, in his tiny two-seater, in my green convertible.
        Moving forward, on a divided highway.

The blackberry vines overrun my garden.
    They suckle from deep roots, choke my cool mint.
        Their red hunger ripens to purple, bursts.

How to Be Deposed

Apply two coats of waterproof mascara.
Floss until it steadies your hands. Sit down
while you sheath your winter legs
in ultra-sheer pantyhose, Nude #2. Remember
the time before your ninth deposition,
teetering in your hallway in a twisted
tree pose, you wrenched your back,
flailing like a netted trout.
Do not bat your eyelashes at your lover,
I mean, lawyer, until you two are alone
in a taxi fleeing the scene.
Don't shriek when plaintiff's counsel
accuses you of sleeping with
the defendant. Try to forget
that co-counsel's son carpools
with your daughter. Count the lines
in the wood grain of the
conference room table. Hum
in your head to the rat-a-tat
of the stenographer's flying fingers.
Breathe. Wait for your lawyer's objection.
Later, when he asks: *Was it true?*
don't slap him. Don't place a straight razor
near your bubble bath. Leave
your pearl-handled revolver at home,
tucked under your monogramed hankies.
Remember you don't have a revolver…
or hankies. Remember all the dimes
you earned ironing your father's hankies.
Try to forget his shadow in your doorway.
Try to forget his hand over your mouth.
Try to forget the sticky touch of your brother's
beanbag chair on your bare thighs,
your brother's threat: *I'll tell everyone what you did.*
Try to forget his needling question:
Does it feel good when I touch you here?

Driving over the I-90 bridge after another flashback

A black SUV muscles past,
      shoves me to the guardrail.

Below, the water calls:
      Come to me. Come to me.
I long to drape my body in its green cloak.

Crossover, crossover,
      keep driving, crossover.
I sing to my steering wheel.

My days a minefield:
      treadmill, radio, oven, TV,
      cherry trees, computer, movie theater.
Flashbacks hide under every bush.

I can't walk softly enough.
I can't erase my face
      in the morning mirror.

A classic Beetle cruises along,
      its blue-green patina sings
      a mermaid song.

I imagine my hair swooning underwater,
dark jellyfish drifting down, down, down.
      Crossover, crossover,
      keep driving, crossover.

My daughter asks and asks:
      Are you okay, Mommy?
Is this how lying starts—
      pinning a smile on Catastrophe?

Maybe I'm a loon in June.
I howl to a mute moon, pale thief
　　　climbing the black rungs of night.

Something shuttered in me after
I gave birth, my body walking
　　　the line between always and never.

Daughter apricot. Son persimmon.
　　　　　Fuzz and slime.
Your children are better off without you,
　　　the lake murmurs, applauding its dead.

I'm lightheaded, my breath held
　　　in a point of light glinting
　　　off my windshield.
Crossover, crossover,
　　　keep driving, crossover.

A few more inhales and I'll soar
　　　with the seagulls,
their arrogant flight, their smirking
　　　caw caw, caw caw.

But no, I'm too heavy.
Today, I am rain.

Queen of Everything

At the theatre gala, I ragdoll in my husband's arms,
     flung and spun, but I can't unsee

my ex-lover's hand on the small of her back.
     Once, I was a river & he was sunlight,

all sparkle & thirst. Now, my peach silk dress flows
     nowhere. I exit for the ladies' room,

praying he will follow, but tonight all I am
     is a silver sandal and he is stairs

devoid of pitch, all flight and no tomorrows.
     If I wanted what I have, I wouldn't be

my father's daughter. I'd be the desk on which
     his bimbo fucked another man.

My father now living under my sister's roof.
     My phone calls echo down the well of her silence.

My ex-lover's hand on the small of her back.
     How She reminds me of my sister: froth of pitch-

black curls, dawn-blue eyes glittering: Mine! So easily
     I forget my waking dreams of childhood,

my father passing me on his way to my younger sister's bed,
     loving her in the night the way he once

loved me, snake eyes and fire breath, crowning her
     queen of everything.

Yom Kippur

Fall tracks footprints
       through rooms too small and numbered,
       floors shouting up naked stairs or down.
We choose our substitutions:
       the faces we hold between our hands
       and kiss with eyes made wide.
The trees shed leaves like green tears.
       Ragged footsteps hurried on the way
       to some bright elevation,
another path to love or to the illusion
       of a mountaintop where breath is deeper,
       hope blooms in a purple crocus.
Everyone's cold. Wine leaks
       from a cracked glass. Fasting promises
       a God who has abandoned me.
I'll bow through days of awe.
       The pendulum swings. I pray
       that someone, somewhere can hear.

Lessons from the Upper Realms

I remember my first time skiing
with my husband when we were still dating,
waking to falling snow, each unique snowflake
praising *Hashem* for the miracle of its creation.

I remember his kind hand wrapping my scarf,
his wave as I slid and stuttered toward the bunny hill,
and how, two days later, he whisked me
up the Big Mountain, launched me on a run
that vaulted over an open gulch. I froze.

Behind me the whir and creak of chairlift, bright drifts
of color, ripples of chatter, and, near my foot,
a red hair ribbon half-buried in snow.

You can do this! he said. *Come on already!* he said.
You're making a scene! he said, then leapt and sped away.

Does each new memory we carve deepen
or obliterate the ones that came before?

The next day, he led me to a double-blue catwalk:
on our right, the mountain's rough face, on our left,
a drop-off. I snowplowed the whole way down,
my bent knees pressed together like hands in prayer.

I never skied with him again, but we married
eighteen months later. 18—*chai*—for life, for luck,
for love.

Now, six months shy of our eighteenth anniversary,
I scan the cloud-strewn sky, searching for the face of God.
My spiritual teachers say we come into this life to learn lessons
we chose in the upper realms. *God,* I ask, *why did I choose
the boot and the back? Why did I call that love?*

The clouds are white and silent. No face of God.
No burning bush.

Incantation

Shadows writhe on white walls.
        Crystals wink and mutter.

The healer, in lotus pose, waits,
in vestments of cotton, his unbound hair
        a frost-nipped tide of honey.

I enter as supplicant and skeptic.
What in me must die so I may live in Spirit?

The blood of my tribe, the bond
of my *mishpucha*, my family, hums
in my veins, but also terror.

Do you have a question you'd like answered?
the healer asks. Questions, questions,
a murder of crows. *Can I go home again?*
        squawks from my mouth.

The ritual of thirteen— my sister's daughter
called before the Ark of our Covenant.
A family reunion looms in my hometown.

She will chant from our Torah,
our tribal tongue hard in her soft mouth,
hard like my father's body,

his hand over my mouth,
his knee on my thigh.
Hard, his rape. Harder, my silence.

This week tolls the anniversary of
my remembering. The healer places
his hand on my heart. A thousand needles.

You have closed yourself off from loving, he says.
Smoke rises from a cone of incense.

He places his hand on my back.
I curl inward. *You are afraid those nearest you*
will stab you in the back.

He places his hand on my left hip.
Burning. *Breathe,* he intones,
breathe. You were hurt as a child,

but you are no longer a child. Your truth
is your sword. He palms my forehead.
When danger threatens, you flee your body.

Breathe, he commands. *Breathe.*
Breathe into your thighs, your hips, your belly.
Your body is your chalice, your strength.

In synagogue, we pray: *My strength cometh from the Lord.*

You have lost your faith in God, he says.
The cone of incense crumbles.
        God has not lost his faith in you.

Tethered

After my divorce, I realized
my fear of heights wasn't vertigo,
but the heady desire to fling
myself over the edge
of anything—
a staircase, an overpass,
a fight.

Is that how I died in a past life?

Is that why I married
a stolid, broad-shouldered man
to tether me to this lifetime,
so I could drape him over me
like the dentist's lead apron,
his density pinning me to our bed,
his strong, blunt hands
holding me,
a helium balloon,
keeping me

from drifting up
to the ceiling,
out of my body,
flying away with Jo Jo,
my imaginary childhood friend,

the one who only breezed through
in the night, in the dark,
to carry me away from the crush
of my father's body?

Open House

They razed my childhood home, dug a dungeon
for a dozen cars, paved over the plush green
frontage to plant a trio of pudgy cherubs, and ringed
the vast entryway with towering Corinthian pillars.

They demolished the green and white-trellised
garden room where we played backgammon and
gutted my mother's beloved flower beds to build
a dining room large enough to host a village.

They wiped out my yellow bedroom linked to my sister's,
but not my rage at her waking me on weekends,
pouncing on me, pinning my arms beneath
her skinny knees, tickling me past my screams.

They annihilated the mudroom with its reek
of turned earth and laundry, but not the memory
of my older brother, his hair frizzed around his face
like an antique gold halo, framed by a white door,
his voice, asking, no, telling me to come upstairs to his room.

They ravaged my parents' master suite, trashed
the velvet-flocked wallpaper, the his and her baths,
but I still hear the echoes of my father's: *You stupid bitch!*
and the slam of my mother's car door.

I wish I could have bulldozed it myself.

When Joy Comes

Don't raise the curtains,
throw a party, invite the neighbors,
set off fireworks. No, spit twice
with furtive glances, left and right,
mutter, *Kina hora*,
your Yiddish grandmother's
invocation against the evil eye.

Your DNA cringes
with the genetic imprint
of Cossacks setting fire
to your Russian ancestors'
wedding party,
grabbing the virgin bride,
yanking her dark rope of hair,
twisting her hooked nose.

The Devil jeers:
Don't be too happy!
The Proverbs warn:
Pride goeth before a fall.
Your mother's punishment:
take away whatever you love most.

You hoard your golden apples
until they wither in your dark cellar.
You drape a tent of rags
around the fire of your poetry
until it suffocates, burns out.
You hang your art inside a citadel,
raise the drawbridge, fill the moat.

And still, friends drift away,
jobs end, lovers betray.

Risk the ricochet of fate,
taunt the gods
with your raucous joy!

If we are to lose everything in this life,
and for sure we will
with our last breath,
then let us rejoice:
blast the trumpets,
dance and love.

Yes, let's love
as if this is all there is,
this half-mad falling for
and falling into,
flying in the face of
Oh no, you don't
and *I told you so.*

Yes, if we are
to lose it all,
then let's first make sure
we have something,
no, everything
to lose.

ADDITONAL ACKNOWLEDGMENTS

Thank you to Rose, Farzaneh, Kay and Heather who offered space and heart for me to voice my unspeakable truths. Thank you to Jack Grapes, my first and always poetry mentor, in whose Method Writing workshop, the *Cheers* of writing classes, many of these poems were birthed. Thank you to Ellen Bass and Laura Davis, whose book, *Courage to Heal*, helped light my path out of the dark silence of repressed memories, and I will be forever grateful for the opportunity to write under your guidance. Thank you to Kim Rosen for teaching me the joy of writing a poem on your bones and speaking it from the heart, for your weaving of poetry, music, breath and movement and for your Poetry Depths Mystery School. Thank you to Tresha Faye Haefner for your Poetry Salon and for your patient editing that helped shape many of these poems. I am so happy to call you *cousin*! And, most of all, a special thanks to my husband, Jon, for ... *everything*: your first review of everything I write, your inspiring me to take my poems out of my journals and into the world, and for being the soil in which I bloom.

Elya Braden was born and raised in Southern California. After seeing *The Sound of Music* when she was four, she began singing and dancing around the living room, then acting and directing her friends in plays. She began writing poems in middle school to navigate puberty and life's other challenges. At 16, she was accepted into an exclusive poetry writing workshop at Harvard University. However, when her first submission to a literary magazine was rejected when she was 18, she lost faith in poetry. She continued to sing and act through college and law school, but never believed in her talents enough to pursue a career on stage.

Instead, Elya took a fourteen-year detour from her creative endeavors to pursue a career as a corporate securities lawyer. She specialized in public offerings, mergers and acquisitions and served as General Counsel of two public companies in Seattle, WA.

After retiring from the law, Elya resumed her love of singing and acting, performing in jazz clubs and cabaret shows, musicals, independent films and TV commercials, which inspired her return to Los Angeles. Once there, she heard the call to "tell her own story instead of playing a role in other people's stories."

Her work has appeared in *Calyx, Forge, Gyroscope Review, poemmemoirstory* (now *Nelle*), *Rattle Poets Respond,* and *Willow Review,* among other publications. She has been a featured reader at Tasty Words, the Rapp Salon and Poetry Fixx and reads at venues throughout Los Angeles.

Following her success publishing her poetry in literary journals and magazines, Elya created and leads workshops for other writers on How to Get Published. As a trained NIA dance instructor and mixed-media artist, she has led workshops interweaving poetry/visual art and poetry/music/movement.

Elya is married to the brilliant short story writer, artist and creativity consultant, Jon Pearson, and they live in West Los Angeles with their now-famous cat, CoCo. Visit Elya online at www.elyabraden.com.